A mirror of tenderness and truth—
this book breathes.

I Was Never the Story

A Poetic Fictional Memoir

Bodhi Dion

I Was Never the Story

This is a poetic fictional memoir.

It is rooted in lived experience, yet names, timelines, scenes, and details have been reshaped, condensed, or reimagined for rhythm, privacy, and the clarity of presence.

Cover and Book Design by Bodhi Dion

www.WakeUpBites.com

ISBN 979-8-9932697-0-2

First Edition

Published by Wake-Up Bites™ Editions

Dedication

For the ones who feel too much,

carry too long,

and wake in the middle of the night

with nothing but breath

and being.

This is not a guide.

It is a mirror.

A Note on the White Pages

Some pages are intentionally left blank.

Nothing is missing.

You may pause—

or not.

Silence also reads.

Author's Note

This book is not about what happened.
It's about what was realized.

It is not chronological.
It does not resolve.
It does not explain.

It is fragments of memory, spirit, and silence—
written not to teach,
but to witness what remains
when the story falls away.

There is no one who sees.
There is only seeing.

Epigraph

"Nobody can hurt you when you are a nobody. You cannot be wounded—because the ego is very ready to receive wounds. The ego is almost seeking and searching to be wounded; it exists through wounds. Its whole existence depends on misery, pain."

—Osho

Contents

The Refrigerator Light

I was standing naked in front of the open fridge
at 3:12 a.m., eating cold spaghetti with my fingers
like it was communion.

The refrigerator light cast this weird, holy glow over
the linoleum floor—divine grace brought to you by
leftover carbohydrates.

There was a moth circling the ceiling light,
tapping the glass like it was trying to get in
or get out.
I couldn't tell which.
It reminded me of therapy.

Or love.
I didn't know then that I had PTSD.
I just thought I was dramatic.
Sensitive. "Too much."

The kind of person who reads the warning label
on a shampoo bottle
and wonders if it's a metaphor.

I lived in an apartment filled with
echoes of unanswered presence,
half-finished journals,
and plants that were trying harder than I was.

There was a yoga mat in the corner
that had only ever been used
to cushion existential crises.

The woman I loved at the time—
let's call her Lucía because that wasn't her name—
said I had "emotional layers."

What she meant was I cried during a cereal
commercial
and once tried to hug a parking meter

because I thought it was a metaphor
for "life being cold and unyielding."

She left after I said,
"I think I don't know how to be loved
without apologizing for it."

She didn't pack much.
Just the books I never read
and a tiny cactus
that had survived our entire relationship without
dying.

I respected the hell out of that cactus.

The Man Who Sold Nothing

There was a man who lived two floors above me

who sold absolutely nothing.

He set up a folding table outside the apartment

every Saturday,

arranged it with precise emptiness,

and sat behind it

sipping mate tea from a gourd.

When people passed by, he'd nod solemnly.

Occasionally, someone would stop and ask,

"What are you selling?"

He'd answer: "Perspective."

They'd laugh.

He wouldn't.

Sometimes I'd watch from my window and think:

God, I wish I had that kind of audacity.

I sold myself for approval every day.
He sat there like someone who had stepped outside
of identity,
offering nothing but space.

He reminded me of my grandfather,
who once told me:
"Don't let people rent space in your head
if they're not paying in kindness."

He also told me that chocolate was a vegetable,
because cocoa beans come from a plant.
He was right about both.

I asked the man once,
"How do you make a living?"

He said: "By losing the need to."

The Plastic Sword

At seven, I carried a plastic sword everywhere,

convinced it could kill ghosts.

It was red and slightly bent,

and I named it: Truth.

I used to sleep with it under my pillow,

just in case the man from the hallway

tried to sneak into my dreams again.

That man wasn't real, I was told.

"Just your imagination."

Except my imagination had hands.

And breath.

One night, I stabbed the dark so hard

the sword snapped in half.

I buried it in the backyard.

Truth died.

And no one came to the funeral but me.

That was the year I stopped believing.

Sofia's Soup

Sofia made this soup
that tasted like forgiveness.
Carrots and ginger and
whatever else she put in it
that I never learned.

I sat at her table
in clothes that didn't belong to the moment,
still holding onto ego like it was armor.

"Let the soup reach your sadness,"
she said once—
like that was normal.

She never asked what had happened to me.
She didn't need to.
She could taste it.

She fed me like I was a stray dog,

starving for meaning.

That soup broke something in me—

gently,

like a window opening.

Letter to a Younger Me

Dear You,

I know you don't trust letters.
They never brought anything good.
They meant boarding school.
Abandonment.
A shift in reality.

But this one is different.

You're not crazy.
You're not broken.
You are reacting
exactly as any human would
to pain.

You will grow into someone who can tell
stories about ghosts—without shaking.

You'll find people who stay.

You'll learn to eat soup
without apologizing for being hungry.

You'll realize
that trauma isn't who you are.
It's just the fire you passed through.
And yes—it burned.
But it didn't end you.

Keep the sword,
even if it's broken.

Love,
You

Stillness After the Storm

The silence after a panic attack

feels like holy ground.

Not relief—

more like surrender.

That's when I began to hear something deeper.

Not a voice.

Not words.

Just...

presence.

The nervous system

can be both the battlefield

and the teacher.

Breathwork

The first time I really breathed—

not out of habit,

but with awareness—

I cried.

In that breath,

I began to meet not a self that reacted—

but presence itself.

Reaction belonged to the conditioned parts of me.

But the witness?

It didn't react.

It simply was.

And from that place,

response could arise—

clean, aware, and unburdened.

Forgiveness Isn't a Feeling

Forgiveness wasn't about saying,

"What happened was okay."

It was about saying,

"I won't let what happened define me anymore."

I forgave

not to free them—

but because I couldn't carry their weight

and my healing

at the same time.

The Edge

There is a place in healing

that feels worse than being unhealed.

It's the edge.

Where you question everything.

Where you sit

with what feels unbearable.

But every time I stayed with it—

really stayed—

I felt something beneath it.

"You're not dying.

You're just awakening."

The Seeing That Frees

It wasn't effort that freed me.

Not healing.

Not knowledge.

It was…seeing.

And in that seeing,

identification began to dissolve.

The ego doesn't die by battle.

It fades

like a dream

when the dreamer wakes.

I Am Not the One Who Hurt

I believed I was the one who was hurt.

The boy.

The failure.

The broken man.

But that was only true

on the surface of being.

The witness?

It wasn't touched.

It knew.

And in that knowing,

compassion flowed.

Beyond Becoming

Healing is useful—

until it's not.

The self that wants to be healed

is the same self

that was never real

to begin with.

I stopped trying to become—

and simply allowed

being

to be.

Silence Has No Opinion

Silence never agreed with me.

Or disagreed.

In silence,

there's no validation.

Just a mirror.

And if you stay long enough,

it reflects nothing.

And somehow,

that nothing

feels more like home

than anything

I ever tried to be.

The Fall of the Doer

For most of my life,

I thought I had to do something

to be okay.

But the "doer"

was just another mask.

A sacred-looking disguise.

A thief dressed as a priest.

The doing didn't lead me home.

The stopping did.

The Simple Freedom of Not Knowing

No longer needing

to name the trauma.

No longer needing

to finish the story.

No longer needing

to understand.

And somehow,

in that unknowing,

there was rest.

Returning Without a Map

The seeker believes there's a path.

A direction.

A goal.

But the one who is awake

sees—

there never was a journey.

We are simply returning

to what was always

already

here.

Munich, Again

I once believed

Munich was a turning point.

But now I see:

there are no turning points.

Even the MDMA *groups*

weren't the cause of awakening.

They were only openings.

The light didn't come from the substance.

It came from the one

who saw

there was never anything

to fix.

Meeting My Son, Once More

I looked into my son's eyes

and saw being

in form.

Not roles.

Not pain.

Just...presence.

In that moment,

something in me

stopped performing.

And I was

simply

here.

The Boutique Never Closed

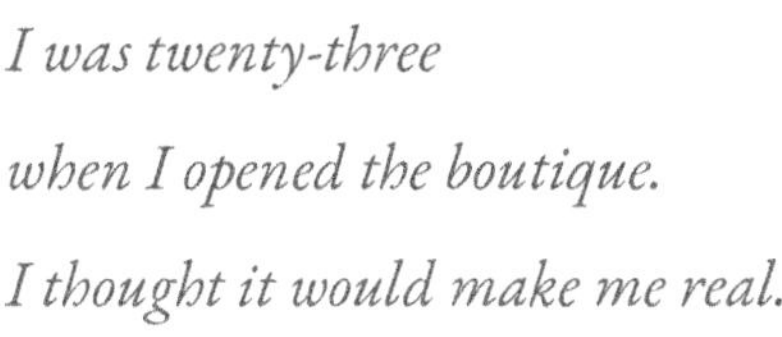

I was twenty-three

when I opened the boutique.

I thought it would make me real.

Models.

Shows.

Loans.

Dreams.

And then—

it fell apart.

But something was revealed.

The boutique never failed.

It delivered its purpose:

to lure the mask into the light.

It never closed.

It dissolved.

The Gift of Exhaustion

Eventually,

even the ego gets tired.

And when it does,

something softer emerges.

I didn't want to improve anymore.

I just wanted to be.

That was the beginning.

The Idea of Me

There's a strange moment in silence

when the mind reaches

for the idea of "me"—

but it can't find it.

What's left isn't void.

It's presence.

After the Storm

What comes after awakening?

Not bliss.

Not perfection.

Just breath.

Dishes.

Grief in old muscles.

But no belief in the story.

No self-clinging to it.

The Door Was Never Locked

The door was never locked.

I just believed I was on the outside.

Fear made it look real.

But presence

dissolves walls without trying.

Not Enlightened, Just Honest

Awakening didn't make me special.

It just made me honest.

No more pretending.

No more performance.

Just truth—

without a costume.

The Spiritual Show

I was still performing—

just in robes now.

Quoting mystics

without naming.

Collecting concepts

like sacred props.

But the ego doesn't care

what it wears.

True silence

stripped all that away.

And I could finally

breathe.

The Big Bang Was Quiet

Awakening didn't explode.

It landed

like a feather.

No more defense.

No more need.

Just a breath

I didn't know I was holding—

released.

No Exit

The exit never existed.

There was no trap.

No outside.

Just presence.

Just this.

Just now.

No rescue.

No escape.

Only the truth:

I am home.

Witnessing

Bodhi Dion has lived many lives.

Some were called artist.

Some were called seeker.

Father.

Lover.

Entrepreneur.

Student.

Academic.

Manager.

And, again, student.

Some roles felt true.

Some were survival.

All were temporary.

None of them remain.

He doesn't claim stillness.

But life keeps reminding him—

in the space between triggers,

and the breath after reaction—

that he is not the story.

He is not writing from finality.

He is writing from witnessing.

This book is not an explanation.

It's a quiet remembering.

Bodhi Dion no longer tells his story.

Not as a beginning or an ending,

but as a gentle echo

of a glimpse

of what was always here.

About the Cover

The white lotus has long symbolized purity, awakening, and rebirth—a flower that emerges from the mud, untouched by it. That paradox has always spoken to me: How something can rise from darkness and remain unsoiled, even luminous. This is the quiet metaphor beneath every page of this book. The lotus grows out of the same mud we try so hard to escape—the pain, the trauma, the confusion. And yet it rises, not in resistance to the mud, but because of it. I chose the white lotus for the cover because it carries what I cannot say directly: That healing does not come from escaping the human condition, but from seeing it—and blooming anyway.

Acknowledgments

To Osho, whose vision opened the way I see and live.
Without it, none of this would have been possible.

These pages would not exist.

To the people who crossed my path—
gently, fiercely, briefly, or for a long time.

Each encounter left a trace
that found its way into this book.

My gratitude is quiet, but real.

Namaste

Bodhi Dion

My life behind this book was rich, intense, and multilayered— impossible to summarize without doing violence to it.

What remains is not a biography,
but a distillation:
the essence without the story.

For years, I moved as if controlled,
shaped by unseen trauma.
I don't look at who I was.
The one I was has dissolved.
I look at what is here.

www.ingramcontent.com/pod-product-compliance
Lightning Source LLC
LaVergne TN
LVHW011048110826
845149LV00015B/3409

* 9 7 9 8 9 9 3 2 6 9 7 0 2 *